Published 2015 by Celebration Press
58 Helen Close
East Finchley
London N2 0UU
UK
celebrationpress3@gmail.com

Designed and typeset in-house

Production: Steph Bramwell

Printed by: CPI London

British Library cataloguing in publication data.
A catalogue record for this book is available from The British Library.

Contents:

The cutting

You took me through the cutting,
across the heath to visit family.

It was early spring,
with a smell of last year's vegetation.

Decades on,
I walk again through the cutting.
It is the end of winter,
and the day is damp,
with a smell of last year's vegetation.

The leafless trees soar in majesty,
fingers pointing to the sky.

The leafless trees soar in majesty
fingers pointing to the sky

2

Renewal

Daffodils in bloom, take me to the garden's end
where blackbirds nest-build in the ivy.

 The snowdrops have gone,
but the primroses shine.

Clematis arches and patient roses
await their flowering.

Everything is as it should be.

but the

primroses

shine

The village

Night

The river is swollen,
has overcome its banks.
Ancient walls survey the chaos.

Mist hangs on distant hills,
and water laps ghosts of a long-gone workhouse.

This feudal land is under threat.

Day

The fresh green fields look new,
and the hills are dark with cloud.

Swallows play across the house,
and the river flows on.

Rothbury

*The fresh green
fields look new,
and the hills are
dark with cloud*

Autumn song

Now is the time of silhouettes and silences,
of clouds copying sun's rays.
But with the falling of the leaves,
autumn turns to winter.

A time of mist,
of leaves that persist.
Then with the falling of the leaves,
autumn turns to winter.

Trees in autumn tell me
why I'm alive!

But with the falling of the leaves,
autumn turns to winter.

The childhood taste
of blackberries picked in haste.

The smell of sun on dusty footpaths
and dung on country lanes.
With colour raining from the trees,
I still smell autumn in November.

Crow and caw, rook and crow,
autumn light before the snow.
Then, with the falling of the leaves,
autumn turns to winter.

*Colour
raining from
the trees*

New Year

Leaves lie cowering under winter's blast.

A late anemone, head held high,
braves the day.

A smell of rain,
and last year's tangle in the hedgerow.

A late anemone, head held high, braves the day

Joy

A missionary, turned healer,
you care for women and us all.
Creating tapestries
of love and blessings.

A Quaker,
you want them all to sing;
dance circles of universal peace.
And put the kettle on
 when they've had enough of sitting in silence.

circles of
universal peace

A winter's morning

The Brent has iced over,
bent in its purpose of not moving.
The birds have stopped singing,
grass and leaves are frost-encrusted.

Pink-faced girls walk by, smiling.
Hunched office workers,
with hands deep in pockets
and steamy breath,
hurry from the bus stop.

grass and leaves are frost-
encrusted

Water (2)

I lean against the wind,
and the waves come back,
and the waves come back.

Lined along the shore
are men, women, children.

Water is our medium,
giant waves take us forward.
Cosmic travel across oceans, seas.

We are linked by horizons
and images of other lands.

And the waves come back,
and the waves come back.

*and the
waves
come back*

On the edge

It was pub life and politics,
CND and marches.

The interrupted swing of Thelonius Monk,
and the dark sounds of Shostakovich.

There was booze and marijuana.

We were 'on the road' with Kerouac,
and 'climbing ladders' with Wittgenstein.

The respectability of church,
an office job, and depression.

Where are you now, June?

May God forgive you,
and forgive me too.   Hampstead

the dark sounds of
Shostakovich

Into love

Along the yellow paved path,
across a flower-strewn road.

Over the rainbow bridge
and into love with you.

Over the rainbow bridge
and into love with you.

A trip to Hull

Thinking what a nice woman you are
I leave your house,
your bed,
and walk in the early
morning light
to the Bakerloo Line
in bedsitter land.

Office blocks, shops,
and local houses
are silhouetted
in the dawn.
I am awed by the sight
but am afraid to stop.
I argue with myself:
'Relax, feel the wonder of the view,
the train's not due…'

At the main-line station,
sleepy, early-morning travellers
amble about as though lost,
reacting slowly
to everything around them.

I buy my ticket, check my train,
get two cups of tea and a sticky bun
to fight the early-morning emptiness.

Gulls overhead,
plane over gulls,
train over rails.
Here am I in the early-morning light
gliding slowly from King's Cross,
not to return till night.

*Gulls
overhead*

And the Desert flowered

In the beginning was the Desert.
Hot, endless, arid.
Round as an orange,
reflecting the Sun.

There were caves in the centre of the Desert,
latticed, reaching upwards.
Full of water,
waiting…

The Sun, who liked his own reflection,
felt it was permanent.
Knew nothing of the caves,
 could not have comprehended.

At night,
Moon showed her cool face.
Turned a blind eye to cracks in the
Desert.
Smiled, as water seeped through.
Laughed, as torrents surged forward.

And in the morning,
Earth appeared.
Sun, perplexed, shone harder
wanting his own reflection.

Dormant seeds flourished,
and the Desert flowered.

Moon showed her cool face

Spring

A yellow time,
an orange and a yellow time.

A blue time,
a mauve and a blue time.

A climbing time,
a gripping and a reaching-for-the-sun time.

A daffodil and cream time.

A white time,
a green and a white time.

A growth time,
a me and a you time.

a reaching-for-the-sun time

Poppies

Standing silently
we check our posture.

We soften…
give attention to our breathing.
In through the nose,
out through the mouth.

We move to the left;
then to the right.

Moving with our ancestors,
we join heaven and earth.

And looking over my shoulder,
I breathe in poppies.

*I breathe
in poppies*

Bubbles for peace

There were reverends and rockers,
housewives and children.

There were old friends and new friends,
politicians, policemen.

There were Christians and Muslims,
communists and Buddhists.

And banners, such banners,
banners for peace.

There were dancers and drummers,
and children in pushchairs.

There were priests and our poets,
and grannies in wheelchairs.
There were students and
stiltwalkers,
and a brave paraplegic.

And a man with his toy gun,
lit by his laughter,
blowing bubbles, such bubbles.
Bubbles for peace.

London Peace March,
February 15th 2003

blowing bubbles, such bubbles.
Bubbles for peace.

Autumn (1)

A smell of smoke,
stillness before leaves fall.
Season's turning.

A smell of smoke

Beacon

Symbol of my hoping and of my despair,
the mallow tree grows,
glows in the early-morning sun.

Cathedral of flowers:
home for birds and house cats,
refuge for fieldmouse and hedgehog.

It stands like a beacon,
guiding me back to base.

the mallow tree grows.....
refuge for fieldmouse and
hedgehog

34

A nice park

'It's a nice park, Dad,'
said the little boy
as he looked with awe
at the Highgate ponds.

'It's the best!'
said his Dad
and they marched towards
the hill and the kites.

and they marched towards the hill and the kites

Evening

We are supper-full, relaxed.
Through the open window,
caught in its own perspective,
hand-sized blue-bird buddleia lift their skirts
in the early evening breeze.

The indoor silence is broken
by village boys' insistent shouts.

Derbyshire

blue-bird buddleia lift
their skirts

Running down the mountain-side

Walking through gardens of hope,
he contemplates his existence.

What is left but contemplation?
Time is an illusion.

He contemplates beauty in all its forms.
Mind, body,
and the poetry of everyday living.

He knows that softness is strength,
that we must guard our wisdom.
And that art is a key to the spirit

Walking through the hills and
chalk,
he sees poplars move like dancers.
Feels the roots of his existence.

And running down the mountain-
side,
thinking with his feet.

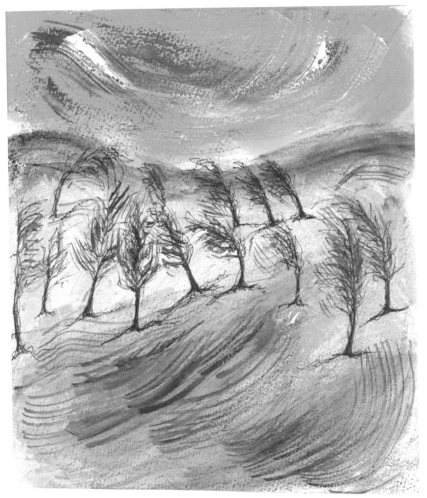

Walking through the hills
and chalk,
he sees poplars move like
dancers.